Windows 10 at the command-line

Quick reference guide to Windows 10's command-line

Part III

About the author

RICCARDO RUGGIU was born in Cagliari in 1976.
He has been working in the silicon-based technology sector for over twenty years, and has gained solid experience working for the most important IT companies in Italy and abroad.
Music has a great impact in his spare time; he is an expert musician (piano, synth and guitar), Dj and deep connoisseur of home and professional audio equipment.

Acknowledgements

Special thanks to my family, and friends, for having always been present.

This book is dedicated to everyone, beginners and experts alike who want to get the most out of their PC and want to explore the maze of the Command Prompt in search of tools and features to coordinate all the operations that the PC does, like a conductor directs all the musicians!

R.Ruggiu

Limit of Liability/Disclaimer of Warranty

Introduction

Dear reader,
welcome to the third part of this quick guide about the command line which, due to the wide variety of arguments and functions, seems to have become a saga! This "third episode" continues the journey inside the black prompt window by examining simple and less simple commands that can help you keep your PC in top shape.
The text is accompanied by practical examples, eloquent explanations and useful suggestions.
Also this book, like the two that preceded it, is divided into three chapters to quickly find what you are looking for (ex. topic "Networks" chapter II) avoiding consulting pages on pages that contain information that is not of interest, with resulting in a waste of time.
The first explains topics and functions in the field of security and verifications; the second, deals with utilities and checks in the context of computer networks.
The third chapter concludes the book by proposing various commands and utilities that can not only help you better master your PC, but also make you enjoy the

experience of using your machine to the fullest even through simple curiosities!

One of the best features of this book is simplicity.

Each topic is explained step by step and anyone can learn how to use the commands quickly and effortlessly.

The best way to learn about the prompt is to use it, so I invite you to repeat the examples you'll find in the book, practicing using the command line.

I just have to wish you good reading and have fun!

Contents

Chapter I
Security and checks: file permissions

Regarding security, it's possible to assign read, write and execute permissions for each file on the system, allowing or not access to users.

When you create a new file, it inherits the permissions of the folder in which it was created.

This utility born as **Cacls** (now deprecated, although still present), starting from the Windows Vista system onwards it has been updated in **lcacls**.

Let's see how to use **Cacls** to assign permissions.

If you want to give the user "Ricky" read-only permission on the "Test.txt" file, type as follows:

C:\>cacls C:\Documents\Test.txt /G Ricky:r

After typing enter, the system will ask you to confirm the operation or not, by typing Y or N and typing enter again.

```
C:\>cacls C:\Documents\Test.txt /G Ricky:r
Are you sure (Y/N)?
```

At the end of the operation, the system will indicate that the command has been completed:

```
C:\>cacls C:\Documents\Test.txt /G Ricky:r
Are you sure (Y/N)?
C:\>processed file C:\Documents\Test.txt /G Ricky:r

C:\>
```

Now, user Ricky has read-only access to the "Test.txt" file.

Here are the access options:

r   read-only access
w   write-only access
c   change-read/write
f   full access

The *Icacls* utility has a number of options listed below:

ICACLS name /save ACLFile [/T] [/C] [/L] [/Q]

ICACLS directory [/substitute SidOld SidNew [...]] /restore ACLFile [/C] [/L] [/Q]

ICACLS name /setowner user [/T] [/C] [/L] [/Q]

ICACLS name /findsid SID [/T] [/C] [/L] [/Q]

ICACLS name /verify [/T] [/C] [/L] [/Q]

ICACLS name /reset [/T] [/C] [/L] [/Q]

ICACLS name [/grant[:r] Sid:perm[...]]
    [/deny Sid:perm [...]]
    [/remove[:g|:d]] SID[...]] [/T] [/C] [/L] [/Q]
    [/setintegritylevel Level:policy[...]]

The list below describes the elements of the command:

name   indicates the name of the file or folder to which the permissions apply.

/save   stores the ACLs.

ACLFile   indicates the name of the file where the ACLs are stored.

Directory   indicates the directory used to perform a task.

/substitute SIDOld SIDNew   indicates that the command replaces the old SID (security identifier) with the new SID.

/restore   restores the contents of the ACL file.

/setowner   change the owner of the specified element.

User   indicates the username that performs a task.

/findsid   Finds all matching names that contain an ACL where the SID is explicitly indicated.

/verify   Finds all files whose ACL is not in canonical form or whose length is inconsinstent with the number of ACEs.

/reset   Replaces the ACLs in all matching files with the default inherited ACLs.

/grant[:r] Sid:perm   grants access rights to the specified user.
With :r, the permissions override any previously granted explicit permissions.
Without :r, the permissions are added to the explicit permissions previously granted.

/deny Sid:perm   explicitly denies rights to the specified user.
An explicit denial access control entry is added to the relevant authorization and the same authorizations are removed from any explicit concessions.

/remove[:[g|d]] **SID** Removes all occurrences of the SID in the ACL.

>   With :g, all occurrences of the rights granted to the SID are removed.
>   With :d, all occurences of the rights denied to the SID are removed.

/setintegritylevel *[(CI)(OI)]Level* Explicitly add an integrity access control entry to all matching files. To specify the level, use one of the following values:

>   L[ow]
>   M[edium]
>   H[igh]

>   Before the level, you can specify the options relating to the inheritance of the integrity access control entry, which are applied only to directories.

/inheritance:e|d|r
> e – Enable inheritance.
> D – Disable inheritance and copy access control entries.
> R – Removes all inherited ACEs.

/T Indicates that the operation is performed on all corresponding files or directories contained in the directories specified in the name.

/C Indicates that the operation must continue even in the event of file errors.
The error messages will still be displayed.

/L Indicates that the operation is performed on the symbolic link itself rather than on its destination.

/Q Indicates that successful messages should not be displayed.

ICACLS maintains the canonical ordering of access control entries:

> Explicit denials
> Explicit grants
> Inherited denials
> Inherited grants

perm is an authorization mask that can be specified in two different ways:

> As a sequence of basic rights:
>> N – No access
>> F – Full access
>> M – Modify access
>> RX – Read and execute access
>> R – Read-only access
>> W – Write-only access
>> D – Delete

As a comma delimited list of specific rights in parentheses:

>> DE – Elimination
>> RC – Read control
>> WDAC – Write DAC
>> WO – Write owner
>> S – Synchronize
>> AS – Access system security
>> MA – Maximum allowed

GR – Generic read
GW – Generic write
GE – Generic execute
GA – Generic all
RD – Read data/list directory
WD – Write data/add file
AD – Append data/add subdirectory
REA – Read extended attributes
WEA – Write extended attributes
X – Execute/traverse
DC – Delete child
RA – Read attributes
WA – Write attributes

Both forms can be preceded by the rights of inheritance, which are applied only to directories:

(OI) – Object inherit
(CI) – Container inherit
(IO) – Inherit only
(NP) – Don't propagate inherit
4 – Authorization inherited from parent container

Restore file authorization

With the **Takeown** command, you can take back ownership of files that you can't access.
If you want to take back ownership of a file, let's see an example together:

Open the command prompt as administrator, and type:

C:\>takeown /F "C:\Test\Test.txt*" /R /A /D S

In this example, we want to take ownership of the "Test.txt" file, which is located in the path indicated below:

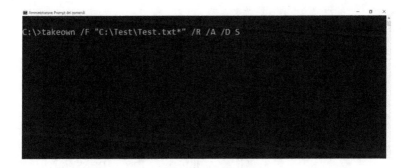

after pressing enter, you'll see the following output:

```
C:\>takeown /F "C:\Test\Test.txt*" /R /A /D S

C:\>SUCCESS: The file (or folder): "C:\Test\Test.txt" now owned by the administ
rators group

C:\>
```

As indicated by the output, the "Test.txt" file is now owned by the Administrators group.

Below is the list of the options for the takeown command:

/S system   Specifies the remote system to connect to.

/U [domain\]user Specifies the user context in which you work within a domain.

/P [password]   Specifies the password for the indicated user context.
If omitted, the password is required.

/F filename   Specifies the file name or directory name pattern you want to own.

/A   Assign ownership of the object to the Administrators group instead of the current user.

/R   Recursive: sets the tool to operate on the specifications of the files present in the specified directory and in all subdirectories

/D prompt   The default answer is used when the current user doesn't have permission to view the contents of the folder in a directory.
This occurs when operating in recursive mode (/R) in subdirectories.
Valid values are "Y" to become owners or "N" to ignore.

/SKIPSL   Do not follow symbolic links.
Only applicable with /R.

Find out information about a user connecting to a remote computer

To view information about a user with access to a remote computer, you can use the **Finger** utility.
Of course, the remote computer must have the finger service running (Linux/Unix).
The command output includes the user name, type of terminal (TTY or teletypewriter), the login name, the total idle time, when and where the user logged in.

The syntax of the command is shown below:

FINGER [-l] [user]@host [...]

Here are the options:

-l   Shows information in a long list format.
User   Specifies the user on whom information is sought.
Omit the parameter to view information about all users on the specified host.

@host   Specifies the server on the remote system on which you are looking for user information.

Checking file type and association

When you click on a file to open it, Windows checks the type of file extension (by file extension we mean those characters that are immediately after the period, in the file name) in order to understand which program it should use to open it:

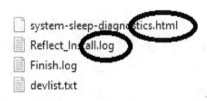

If you don't see the file extension, select the "File name extensions" check box in the "view" tab as indicated below:

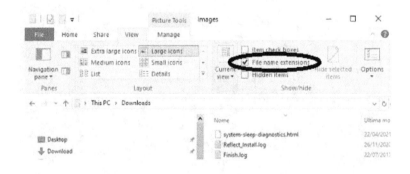

For example, if Microsoft Word is installed on your PC, to open a file with the extension ".doc" it will use the Microsoft Word program since, as mentioned earlier, Windows always checks which program is associated with a file based on its extension.

The **Assoc** utility allows you to see (or change) the association between the file extension and the file type.

```
C:\>assoc
```

To check the type of extension, type assoc followed by the file extension (also typing the dot) you want to check as indicated in the example below:

```
C:\>assoc .doc
.doc=Word.Document.8

C:\>assoc .exe
.exe=exefile

C:\>assoc .txt
.txt=txtfile

C:\>assoc .xls
.xls=Excel.Sheet.8

C:\>assoc .pdf
.pdf=AcroExch.Document.DC

C:\>
```

The command output indicates both the file extension and the type of file to which that extension is associated.
If you want to know more details, you can write assoc again followed by the part after the same symbol of the output received:

```
C:\>assoc .iso
.iso=Windows.IsoFile

C:\>assoc Windows.IsoFile
Windows.IsoFile=Disc Image File

C:\>assoc .pdf
.pdf=AcroExch.Document.DC

C:\>assoc AcroExch.Document.DC
AcroExch.Document.DC=Adobe Acrobat Document

C:\>
```

In the command output, you can see that it's a disk image and then an Adobe Acrobat document.
The *Assoc* command helps you to trace the type of program to use to open a file, when you do not know what the extension of a file refers to and even Windows cannot open it.

The syntax of the command is shown below:

ASSOC [.ext[=[FileType]]]

.ext   Specifies the file extension with which to associate the file type.

FileType   Specifies the type of file to associate with the file extension.

To proceed with the association, for example, of the ".exe" extension with the "exe" file type, type as follows and press enter:

C:\>assoc .exe=exefile

Below is the output:

```
Amministratore: Prompt dei comandi                                    -  □  ×

C:\>assoc .exe=exefile
.exe=exefile

C:\>
```

To view the full list of current associations on your computer, simply type *Assoc* and hit enter; below is a part of the long list of associations, generated by the command output:

```
Amministratore: Prompt dei comandi                                    –  ☐  ×
C:\>assoc
.386=vxdfile
.3g2=WMP11.AssocFile.3G2
.3ga=VLC.3ga
.3gp=WMP11.AssocFile.3GP
.3gp2=WMP11.AssocFile.3G2
.3gpp=WMP11.AssocFile.3GP
.5vw=wireshark-capture-file
.669=VLC.669
.a52=VLC.a52
.AAC=WMP11.AssocFile.ADTS
.accda=Access.ACCDAExtension.12
.accdb=Access.Application.12
.accdc=Access.ACCDCFile.12
.accde=Access.ACCDEFile.12
.accdr=Access.ACCDRFile.12
.accdt=Access.ACCDTFile.12
.accdu=Access.WizardUserDataFile.12
.accountpicture-ms=accountpicturefile
.acl=ACLFile
```

Managing the link between the file type and the program that runs it

To manage the link between the file type and the program that runs it, you can use the **Ftype** (File Type) utility.

```
C:\>ftype
```

By typing ftype followed by the file type, the command generates an output that includes the file type and the complete path to the executable file of the application that allows you to open and / or view it.

In this example, let's see how you can check the file type and check the default path to the program's executable file to open it, using the *Assoc* command (seen earlier) and then *Ftype*:

```
C:\>assoc .pdf
.pdf=AcroExch.Document.DC

C:\>ftype AcroExch.Document.DC
AcroExch.Document.DC="C:\Program Files (x86)\Adobe\Acrobat Reader DC\Reader
\AcroRd32.exe" "%1"

C:\>
```

Let's analyze the output together:

C:\>assoc .pdf
.pdf=AcroExch.Document.DC

Copy the file type (all the part after the equal symbol) and after typing ftype, paste and press enter.

C:\>ftype AcroExch.Document.DC
AcroExch.Document.DC="C:\Program Files (x86)\Adobe \Acrobat Reader DC\Reader\AcroRd32.exe" "%1"

After the equal symbol, you can see the link path to the executable file of the Acrobat Reader program, which allows you to open files with the ".pdf" extension.

The utility uses the following syntax:

FTYPE [FileType[=[OpenCommandString]]]

FileType   Specifies the file type to view or modify.

OpenCommandString   Specifies the opening command
                      to be used for execution of the
                      indicated file.

To view all file types for which command strings are currently defined on your computer, simply type *Ftype* and press enter.

Below is a part of the command output:

```
Amministratore: Prompt dei comandi                                    -  o  x

C:\>ftype
Access.ACCDAExtension.12=C:\PROGRA~2\MICROS~1\Office12\MSACCESS.EXE /NOSTAR
TUP "%1"
Access.ACCDCFile.12="C:\Program Files (x86)\Microsoft Office\Office12\MSACC
ESS.EXE" /NOSTARTUP "%1"
Access.ACCDEFile.12="C:\Program Files (x86)\Microsoft Office\Office12\MSACC
ESS.EXE" /NOSTARTUP "%1" %2 %3 %4 %5 %6 %7 %8 %9
Access.ACCDRFile.12="C:\Program Files (x86)\Microsoft Office\Office12\MSACC
ESS.EXE" /RUNTIME "%1" %2 %3 %4 %5 %6 %7 %8 %9
Access.ACCDTFile.12="C:\Program Files (x86)\Microsoft Office\Office12\MSACC
ESS.EXE" /NOSTARTUP "%1"
Access.ADEFile.12="C:\Program Files (x86)\Microsoft Office\Office12\MSACCES
S.EXE" /NOSTARTUP "%1" %2 %3 %4 %5 %6 %7 %8 %9
Access.Application.12="C:\Program Files (x86)\Microsoft Office\Office12\MSA
CCESS.EXE" /NOSTARTUP "%1" %2 %3 %4 %5 %6 %7 %8 %9
Access.BlankDatabaseTemplate.12="C:\Program Files (x86)\Microsoft Office\Of
fice12\MSACCESS.EXE" /NOSTARTUP /NEWDB "%1"
```

View a detailed report on existing policies

To obtain detailed information on existing policies on a user on a computer (RsoP – Resultant Set of Policy), you can use the **Gpresult** utility.

By typing the *gpresult* utility with */r* option, you can see a summary of the RsoP data.

Below is the output:

C:\>gpresult /R

RSOP data for DESKTOP- E7A4\Ricky on DESKTOP-E7A4 : Logging Mode

OS Configuration:	Standalone Workstation
OS Version:	10.0.19043
Site Name:	N/A
Roaming Profile:	N/A
Local Profile:	C:\Users\Ricky
Connected over a slow link?:	No

USER SETTINGS

Last time Group Policy
was applied: 23/09/2021 at 03:02:05 PM
Group Policy was applied from: N/A
Group Policy slow link threshold: 500 kbps
Domain Name: DESKTOP- E7A4
Domain Type: <Local computer>
Applied Group Policy Objects

N/A

The following GPOs were not applied because they were
filtered out

Local Group Policy
Filtering: Not Applied (Empty)

The computer is a part of the following security groups

BUILTIN\Administrators
Everyone
NT AUTHORITY\Authenticated Users
System Mandatory Level

USER SETTINGS

Last time Group Policy
was applied: 23/09/2021 at 03:02:08 PM
Group Policy was applied from: N/A
Group Policy slow link
threshold: 500 kbps
Domain Name: DESKTOP- E7A4
Domain Type: <Local Computer>

Applied Group Policy Objects

    N/A

The following GPOs were not applied because they were filtered out
----
    Local Group Policy
    Filtering: Not Applied (Empty)

The user is a part of the following security groups

None
        Everyone
        Local account and member of Administrators group
        BUILTIN\Administrators
        BUILTIN\Users
        NT AUTHORITY\INTERACTIVE
        CONSOLE LOGON
        NT AUTHORITY\Authenticated Users
        This Organization
        Local account
        LOCAL
        NTLM Authentication
        High Mandatory Level

C:\>

The syntax of the command is shown below:

Parameter list:

/S system   Specifies the remote system to connect
                 to.

/U [domain\]user   Specifies the user context in
                       which to execute the command

/P [password]   Specifies the password for the
                    indicated user context.
                    If omitted, the password is
                    required.

/SCOPE   Specifies wheter or not to display
               user or computer settings.
               Valid values: "USER",
               "COMPUTER".

/USER [domain\]user   Specifies the username for
                       Which to view resultant set of
                       policy data.

/R   View resultant set of policy summary data.

/V   Shows verbose information.
This information provides additional
Settings that are been applied with
a precedence of 1.

/Z   Specifies very verbose information.
This information provides additional
detailed settings that have been applied
with a precedence of 1 and higher.
In this way it's possible to determine if a
setting has been specified in multiple
locations.

Searching for information within a file

To search for information within a file, you have two utilities; *Find* and *Findstr*.

For example, if you want to search for the word "STORAGE" in the devlist.txt file, type as indicated below:

C:\>find "STORAGE" devlist.txt

Below is the output:

```
Amministratore: Prompt dei comandi                                          –  □  ×
C:\>find "STORAGE" devlist.txt

---------- DEVLIST.TXT
STORAGE\VOLUME\{82E1EDA6-6EF8-11E7-A0E9-806E6F6E6963}#0000000010500000
STORAGE\VOLUME\{82E1EDA6-6EF8-11E7-A0E9-806E6F6E6963}#0000000000100000
STORAGE\VOLUME\{82E1EDA6-6EF8-11E7-A0E9-806E6F6E6963}#000000743EC00000
STORAGE\VOLUME\{82E1EDA6-6EF8-11E7-A0E9-806E6F6E6963}#0000000011500000
```

IMPORTANT: when you type the word to be verified, write it in capital letters or non-capital letters exactly as it's written in the file where you're searching for it.

The syntax of the command is shown below:

/V   Displays lines NOT containing the specified string.

/C	Displays only the count of lines containing the string.
/N	Displays the numbers of the displayed lines.
/I	Ignore uppercase/lowercase letters when searching for the string.
/OFF[LINE]	It doesn't ignore files in which the offline attribute is set.
"string"	Specifies the text string to search for.
[drive:][path]filename	Specifies one or more files to search for.

The *Findstr* utility, supports a more powerful search than the *Find* utility, as it can search for a text string in a file or accross multiple files.

If you want to search for a text string such as "Motherboard resources" in the devlist.txt file, type as follows:

C:\>findstr "Motherboard resources" devlist.txt

If you don't remember which file the string "Motherboard resources" is in, you can extend the search to all files in a folder by typing *.* as in the example below:

C:\>findstr "Motherboard resources" *.*

Below is the output:

```
Amministratore: Prompt dei comandi                                    -  □  ×

C:\>findstr "Motherboard resources" *.*
devlist.txt:    Name: Motherboard resources
devlist.txt:    Name: Motherboard resources
FINDSTR: Impossibile aprire DumpStack.log.tmp
FINDSTR: Impossibile aprire hiberfil.sys
FINDSTR: Impossibile aprire pagefile.sys
FINDSTR: Impossibile aprire swapfile.sys
Test.txt:    Name: Motherboard resources
Test.txt:    Name: Motherboard resources
```

Upon checking the output, the string "Motherboard resources" was found on multiple files.

View the structure of a directory

If you want to "take a picture" inside a directory, you can use the **Tree** utility.

Go to the directory you want to see, type *tree* and press enter:

C:\Windows>tree

Below is a part of the generated output:

Below is the syntax of the command:

TREE [drive:][path] [/F] [/A]

/F Displays the names of the files in each folder.
/A Use ASCII characters instead of extended characters.

Management of mini-filter driver

The *FltMC* (Filter Manager Control) utility, checks the mini-filter drivers on storage hardware such as your Hard Disk Drive.

Mini-filter drivers are useful for defending against viruses as they process filesystem activities including background processes.

I recommend using this utility in two cases: if you want to see which ones are running on the system:

C:\>fltmc.exe

Below is the output:

```
C:\>fltmc.exe

Filter Name                          Num Instances  Altitude   Frame
-----------------------------------  -------------  ---------  -----
bindflt                                  1          409800       0
KLIF                                     7          320400       0
storqosflt                               0          244000       0
wcifs                                    1          189900       0
CldFlt                                   0          180451       0
FileCrypt                                0          141100       0
luafv                                    1          135000       0
klbackupflt                              5          100800       0
npsvctrig                                1           46000       0
Wof                                      4           40700       0
FileInfo                                 6           40500       0
```

This way you can check that there are no anomalies caused by viruses.

Or if the storage hardware manufacturer has released updates that you need to manually install.

The command syntax is as follows:

fltmc load	Load a filter driver.
Fltmc unload	Download a filter driver.
Fltmc filters	Lists the filters currently registered in the system.
Fltmc instances	Lists instances of a filter or volume currently registered on the system.
Fltmc volumes	Lists all volumes /RDRs present on the system.
Fltmc attach	Create a filter instance on a volume
fltmc detach	Removes a filter instance from a volume.

Configure BitLocker Drive Encryption on disk volumes

To proceed with the BitLocker configuration, you can use the *manage-bde* utility.
To check the status, you can type as below:

C:\>manage-bde –status

Below is the output:

C:\>manage-bde –status

Disk volumes that can be protected with BitLocker Drive Encryption
Volume C: [OS]
[OS Volume]

Size :	444,97 GB
BitLocker Version:	None
Conversion Status:	Fully Decrypted
Percentage Encrypted:	0,0%
Encryption Method:	None
Protection Status:	Protection Off
Lock Status:	Unlocked
Identification Field:	None
Key Protectors:	None Found

By checking the output, you can see that at this moment, BitLocker is disabled.

Below is the syntax of the command:

-status   Returns information about volumes eligible for BitLocker.

-on   Encrypt the volume and turn on BitLocker protection.

-off   Decrypt the volume and disable BitLocker protection.

-pause   Suspend encryption, decryption, or wiping of available space.

-resume   Resumes encryption, decryption or wiping of available space.

-lock   Prevents access to data encrypted by BitLocker.

-unlock   Allows access to encrypted data via BitLocker.

-autounlock   Manages automatic unlocking of data volumes.

-protectors   Manages the security methods for the encryption key.

-SetIdentifier or **-si**   Configure the identification field for a volume.

-ForceRecovery or **-fr**   Force recovery when booting a BitLocker-protected operating system.

-changepassword   Change the password for a data volume.

-changepin   Change the PIN for a volume.

-changekey   Change the startup key for a volume.

-KeyPackage o **–kp**   Generate a key package for a volume.

-upgrade   Update the BitLocker version.

-WipeFreeSpace o **–w**   Erase the available space on the volume.

-ComputerName   o   **–cn**   It   runs   on   another computer. Examples: "ComputerX", "127.0.0.1"

IMPORTANT: before using this utility, I recommend that you do some tests on a test computer.

In any case, make sure you always have a backup of your data.

Chapter II Networks: configurations and checks
Management of the Address Resolution Protocol

The *Arp* (Address Resolution Protocol) utility is a useful tool for viewing and editing the tables that are generated when network connections are made.

The Arp protocol manages the association between IP addresses and Mac Addresses (physical addresses) of the interfaces of network devices and computers connected to the network.

By typing the command: C:\>arp –a

you can view current requests:

```
C:\>arp -a
Interface: 192.168.1.17 --- 0x14
  Internet Address      Physical Address      Type
  192.168.1.1           9c- 7- 6-05- 9-b3     dynamic
  192.168.1.255         ff-ff-ff-ff- f- f     static
  224.0.0.2             01-00-5e-00-00- 2     static
  224.0.0.22            01-00-5e-00-00- 6     static
  224.0.0.113           01-00-5e-00-00- 1     static
  224.0.0.251           01-00-5e-00-00- b     static
  224.0.0.252           01-00-5e-00-00- c     static
```

In the command output, you can view the IP address of the interface, the internet address, the physical address (or Mac Address) and the method (Type) of assigning the IP address (static, or dynamic).

This utility uses the following syntax:

ARP –s inet_addr eth_addr [if_addr]
ARP –d inet_addr [if_addr]
ARP –a [inet_addr] [-N if_addr] [-v]

Below is the list of commands available for the arp utility:

-a   View current ARP requests by getting them
            from protocol data. If inet_addr is specified,
            only the IP and physical addresses of the
            specified computer will be displayed. If there
            are multiple network interfaces that use
            ARP, the entries for each ARP table will be
            displayed.

-g   It performs the same task as the –a option.

-v   View current ARP entries in verbose mode.
            All invalid entries and entries related to the
            loopback interface are also displayed.

Inet _addr Specify an internet address.

-N if_addr Displays the ARP entries for the network
            interface specified by if_addr.

-d   Delete the host specified by inet_addr. In
            inet_addr, you can use the asterisk (*)
            wildcard character to delete all hosts.

-s   It adds a new host and associates the inet_addr
              internet address with the physical address
              eth_addr.

              The entry is permanent.

Eth_addr   Specify a physical address. The physical
              address is a hexadecimal number of 6 bytes
              separated by dashes. You can also get the mac-
              address using the _GetMac_ utility.

If_addr   If present, specify the internet address of the
              interface whose address translation table you
              want to change.

              You can also get the IP address using the
              IpConfig utility.

View information on Multicast Routing

To view information on Multicast Routing, you can use the **Mrinfo** utility.

The output of this utility generates a table that includes the interfaces of multicast router (router that checks which groups are active, "polling" the members within its domain every minute) and also the list of machines / devices neighbors.

The syntax of the command is shown below:

mrinfo [-n?] [-i address] [-t secs] [-r retries] destination

The options are as follows:

-n   Displays IP addresses in numeric format
-i   Displays the address of the local interface for sending queries.
-t seconds   Timeout in seconds for IGMP queries (default = 3 secondi)
-r retries   Number of attempts to send SNMP queries (default = 0)
-?   Use print destination address or name

Filter the network traffic and generate a report

Microsoft has added a diagnostic tool for filtering data traffic.
Open Command Prompt in Admin Mode, enter the netsh context and then access the wfp context (**WFP-Windows Filtering Platform**), following the steps below:

C:\>netsh
netsh>wfp
netsh wfp>

Type the **show netevents** command as in the example and press enter:

The command generates a report in ".xml" format as indicated by the command output:

Below is an extract from the report generator:

```
<?xml version="1.0" encoding="UTF-8" standalone="true"?>
<netEvents numItems="77">
  <item>
    <header>
      <timeStamp>2021-09-26T19:58:53.248Z</timeStamp>
      <flags numItems="6">
        <item>FWPM_NET_EVENT_FLAG_IP_PROTOCOL_SET</item>
        <item>FWPM_NET_EVENT_FLAG_LOCAL_ADDR_SET</item>
        <item>FWPM_NET_EVENT_FLAG_REMOTE_ADDR_SET</item>
        <item>FWPM_NET_EVENT_FLAG_LOCAL_PORT_SET</item>
        <item>FWPM_NET_EVENT_FLAG_REMOTE_PORT_SET</item>
        <item>FWPM_NET_EVENT_FLAG_IP_VERSION_SET</item>
      </flags>
      <ipVersion>FWP_IP_VERSION_V4</ipVersion>
      <ipProtocol>6</ipProtocol>
      <localAddrV4>192.168.1.17</localAddrV4>
      <remoteAddrV4>216.58.198.34</remoteAddrV4>
      <localPort>60965</localPort>
      <remotePort>443</remotePort>
      <scopeId>0</scopeId>
      <appId/>
      <userId/>
      <addressFamily>FWP_AF_INET</addressFamily>
      <packageSid/>
      <enterpriseId/>
      <policyFlags>0</policyFlags>
      <effectiveName/>
    </header>
    <type>FWPM_NET_EVENT_TYPE_CLASSIFY_DROP</type>
    <classifyDrop>
      <filterId>94755</filterId>
      <layerId>13</layerId>
      <reauthReason>0</reauthReason>
      <originalProfile>0</originalProfile>
      <currentProfile>0</currentProfile>
      <msFwpDirection>MS_FWP_DIRECTION_IN</msFwpDirection>
      <isLoopback>false</isLoopback>
      <vSwitchId/>
```

43

In the example of the previous pages, I have shown the various steps (*netsh* and *wfp*) to inform you that this command "passes through" two different contexts.
To be faster, you can type everything in the same line and press enter, as shown below:

C:\>netsh wfp show netevents

```
C:\>netsh wfp show netevents
Data collection successful; output = netevents.xml

C:\>
```

Configure a proxy server

To configure a proxy server by command line, open the prompt in administrator mode, log into the netsh context and then the WinHTTP context as follows:

C:\>netsh
netsh>winhttp
netsh winhttp>

Type the command **set proxy** followed by the IP address of the proxy server and the port number as in the example below and press enter:

netsh winhttp>set proxy 118.96.190.181:3128

The output generated by the command will show you the WinHTTP proxy set according to the specified IP address and port.

In the example of the previous pages, I have shown the various steps (*netsh* and *winhttp*) to inform you that this command "passes through" two different contexts.
To be faster, you can type everything in the same line and press enter, as follows:

C:\>netsh winhttp set proxy 118.96.190.181:3128

To check if there is a proxy server configured on the PC or not, type the following command from the netsh context and press enter:

*netsh> **winhttp show proxy***

If you are not inside the **netsh** context, type directly as follows:

C:\>***netsh winhttp show proxy***

Below is the output:

```
Administrator Command Prompt                                    -  □  ×
C:\>netsh winhttp show proxy

Current WinHTTP proxy settings:

    Direct access (no proxy server).
```

The output clearly indicates wheter or not a proxy is
configured on the PC.

View the list of nearby Wi-Fi networks and their details

To view the list of nearby wireless networks, open the command prompt as administrator, type as follows and press enter:

C:\>netsh
netsh>wlan
netsh wlan>

Type the command **show networks mode=bssid** as in the example below and press enter:

netsh wlan>show networks mode=bssid

Below, the command output:

```
netsh wlan>show networks mode=bssid
```

Interface Name: Wi-Fi
There are 4 networks currently visible.

```
SSID 1 : Sitecom
    Network type         : Infrastructure
    Authentication       : WPA2-Personal
    Encryption           : CCMP
    BSSID 1              :  8:0d: 7:2e: 7: 1
        Signal           : 14%
        Radio type       : 802.11n
        Channel          : 4
        Basic rates (Mbps) : 1 2 5.5 11
        Other rates (Mbps) : 6 9 12 18 24 36 48 54

SSID 2 : FRITZ!Box 7530 SN
    Network type         : Infrastructure
    Authentication       : WPA2-Personal
    Encryption           : CCMP
    BSSID 1              : 3 :a6:2 :c5:b  : 5
        Signal           : 10%
        Radio type       : 802.11ac
        Channel          : 1
        Basic rates (Mbps) : 1 2 5.5 6 11 12 24
        Other rates (Mbps) : 9 18 36 48 54
```

SSID 3 : Netgear
   Network type   : Infrastructure
   Authentication   : WPA3-Personal
   Encryption   : CCMP
   BSSID 1   : c:3e: 3:91: 6: 5
      Signal   : 100%
      Radio type   : 802.11ax
      Channel   : 8
   Basic rates (Mbps) : 1 2 5.5 11
   Other rates (Mbps) : 6 9 12 18 24 36 48 54

SSID 4 : D-Link
   Network type   : Infrastructure
   Authentication   : WPA2-Personal
   Encryption   : CCMP
   BSSID 1   : 0:0c: 6:53: 8: 5
      Signal   : 100%
      Radio type   : 802.11n
      Channel   : 7
   Basic rates (Mbps) : 1 2 5.5 11
   Other rates (Mbps) : 6 9 12 18 24 36 48 54

netsh wlan>

In the example of the previous pages, I have shown the various steps (*netsh* and *wlan*) to inform you that this command "passes through" two different contexts.

To be faster, you can type everything in the same line and press enter, as follows:

C:\>netsh wlan show networks mode=bssid

```
C:\>netsh wlan show networks mode=bssid

Interface name : Wi-Fi
There are 4 networks currently visible.

SSID 1 :            771
    Network type          : Infrastructure
    Authentication        : WPA2-Personal
    Encryption            : CCMP
```

Retrieve the password of the Wi-Fi network in use on the computer

It may happen that you forget the Wi-Fi password and have to enter it on a new device, or have to find the Wi-Fi password on another person's computer.
First of all, get the Wi-Fi network name as explained earlier.

Next open the command prompt as administrator, type as follows and press enter:

C:\>netsh
netsh>wlan
netsh wlan>

Type the command **show profile name=Netgear key=clear** as in the example below and press enter:

netsh wlan>show profile name=Netgear key=clear

```
netsh wlan>show profile name=Netgear key=clear
```

Naturally, <u>in the command you'll have to indicate the name of the network to which your PC is connected instead of Netgear</u>.

The command output is shown below, highlighting the password field under *"Key content"*:

Profile Netgear on interface Wireless Network Connection:

Applied: All User Profile

Profile information

Version	: 1
Type	: Wireless LAN
Name	: Netgear
Control options	:
Connection mode	: Connect automatically
Network broadcast	: Connect only if this network is broadcasting

AutoSwitch   : Do not switch to other networks
MAC Randomization : Disabled

Connectivity settings

Number of SSID	: 1
SSID name	: "Netgear"
Network type	: Infrastructure
Radio type	: [Any Radio Type]
Vendor extension	: Not present

Security settings

Authentication	: WPA2-Personal
Cipher	: CCMP
Authentication	: WPA2-Personal
Cipher	: GCMP
Security key	: Present
Key Content	: Ae@=Syf*C2d!P3n6HJP=$9~K!7

Cost settings

Cost	: Unrestricted
Congested	: No
Approaching Data Limit	: No

Over Data Limit	: No
Roaming	: No
Cost Source	: Default

Again, I have shown the various steps (*netsh* and *wlan*) to inform you that this command "passes through" two different contexts.

To be faster, you can type everything in the same line (replacing the network name "Netgear" with the one of your network) and press enter, as follows:

C:\>netsh wlan show profile name=Netgear key=clear

Configure DNS servers addresses

To configure the DNS servers addresses, open the command prompt as administrator and access the netsh context.

Type the following command and press enter to see the available interfaces and verify the correct name of the one you need to configure:

netsh>interface ip show config

Let's assume that the name of the interface to be configured is "*Ethernet*". There are two DNS servers addresses; the *Preferred* one and the *Alternate* one. (in the example, Google's DNS servers)

To configure the *Preferred* one, type as below and press enter:

netsh>*interface ip set dns "Ethernet" static 8.8.8.8*

for the *Alternate* one, type:

netsh>*interface ip add dns "Ethernet" 8.8.4.4 index=2*

From a quick check of the graphical interface, the DNS

are configured correctly:

Remember to write the correct name of the interface, replacing the "Ethernet" one in the example.

Configure a static or dynamic ip address

If you are a system administrator, take care of technical assistance or want to learn how to configure the IP address of a computer at the speed of light... these commands are for you!

First, check the interface name by opening the command prompt window as administrator and typing the following command:

C:\>netsh interface ip show config

Below is the output:

In this case, the interface name is "Ethernet".

Let's see together an example with data given below:

IP address 192.168.0.5
Subnet mask=255.255.255.0
Gateway=192.168.0.1

Below is the command to set the *static IP address*:

C:\>netsh interface ip set address name="Ethernet"
source=static addr=192.168.0.5 mask=255.255.255.0
gateway=192.168.0.1

Repeat the command to view the interface status, to verify that the system has been configured correctly:

C:\>netsh interface ip show config

The output below confirms that the data has been configured correctly.

```
C:\>netsh interface ip show config

Configuration for interface "Ethernet"
    DHCP enabled:                          No
    IP Address:                            192.168.0.5
    Subnet Prefix:                         192.168.1.0/24 (mask 255.255.2
55.0)
    Default Gateway:                       192.168.0.1
    Gateway Metric:                        1
    InterfaceMetric:                       35
    Statically Configured DNS Servers:     None
    Register with which suffix:            Primary only
    Statically Configured WINS Servers:    None
```

Even a quick look at the graphical interface confirms the
correct setting of the static IP address:

Network Connections

→ ∨ ↑ 🖳 › Control Panel › Network and Interr

🖳 Ethernet Properties   ✕

Networking Sharing

Internet Protocol Version 4 (TCP/IPv4) Properties

General

You can get IP settings assigned automatically if your network support
this capability. Otherwise, you need to ask your network administrator
for the appropriate IP settings.

◯ Obtain an IP address automatically

🔘 Use the following IP address:

IP address: 192 . 168 . 0 . 5

Subnet mask: 255 . 255 . 255 . 0

Default gateway: 192 . 168 . 0 . 1

◯ Obtain DNS server address automatically

🔘 Use the following DNS server addresses:

Preferred DNS server: .   .   .

Alternate DNS server: .   .   .

And here is the command to configure the *DHCP (Dynamic Host Configuration Protocol)*, that is the automatic assignment mode (**dynamic IP address**) of the IP address.

Below is the command:

C:\>netsh interface ip set address name="Ethernet" source=dhcp

Verify that the configuration was successful:

C:\>netsh interface ip show config

The output below, <u>confirms that DHCP is enabled</u>, and therefore the automatic IP assignment mode has been configured successfully:

```
C:\>netsh interface ip show config

Configuration for interface "Ethernet"
    DHCP enabled:                         Yes
    IP Address:                           192.168.1.17
    Subnet Prefix:                        192.168.1.0/24 (mask 255.255.255
.0)
    Default Gateway:                          192.168.1.1
    Gateway Metric:                           0
    InterfaceMetric:                          35
    DNS servers configured through DHCP:  192.168.1.1
    Register with which suffix:           Primary only
    WINS servers configured through DHCP: None
```

The graphic interface also confirms the change:

Network Connections

Control Panel > Network and Inter

Ethernet Properties   X

Networking

Internet Protocol Version 4 (TCP/IPv4) Properties

General   Alternate Configuration

You can get IP settings assigned automatically if your network suppor
this capability. Otherwise, you need to ask your network administrato
for the appropriate IP settings.

◉ Obtain an IP address automatically

◯ Use the following IP address:

IP address: .   .   .

Subnet mask: .   .   .

Default gateway: .   .   .

◉ Obtain DNS server address automatically

◯ Use the following DNS server addresses:

Preferred DNS server: .   .   .

Alternate DNS server: .   .   .

Increase browsing speed

If you're experiencing slow navigation problems, you can try to disable the "*Receive Window Auto-Tuning Level or Autotuning*":

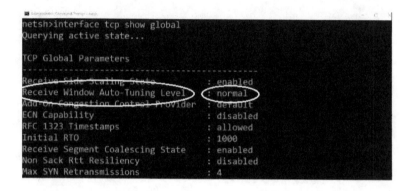

In some cases, this feature can slow down browsing.
To disable *Autotuning*, open the command prompt as administrator, type the following command and press enter:

netsh>interface tcp set global autotuninglevel=disabled

The output below confirms that *Autotuning* is disabled:

```
netsh>interface tcp show global
Querying active state...

TCP Global Parameters
----------------------------------------------------
Receive-Side Scaling State            : enabled
Receive Window Auto-Tuning Level      : disabled
Add-On Congestion Control Provider    : default
ECN Capability                        : disabled
RFC 1323 Timestamps                   : allowed
Initial RTO                           : 1000
Receive Segment Coalescing State      : enabled
Non Sack Rtt Resiliency               : disabled
Max SYN Retransmissions               : 4
```

Restart the computer to complete the operation.

To re-enable *Autotuning*, type the following command and press enter:

netsh><u>interface tcp set global autotuninglevel=normal</u>

```
netsh>interface tcp set global autotuninglevel=normal
Ok.

netsh>
```

Restart the computer to complete the operation.

Transform your PC into an emergency Wi-Fi access point

Before starting, we need an important premise; not all Wi-Fi network cards allow this configuration.

To check, open command prompt as administrator, type as below and press enter:

C:\>netsh wlan show drivers

Below, the output of the command:

```
netsh>wlan show drivers

Interface name: Wi-Fi

    Driver                          : Qualcomm Atheros AR956x Wireless Network
Adapter
    Vendor                          : Qualcomm Atheros Communications Inc.
    Provider                        : Microsoft
    Date                            : 3/26/2016
    Version                         : 3.0.2.201
    INF file                        : athw8x.inf
    Type                            : Native Wi-Fi Driver
    Radio types supported           : 802.11b 802.11g 802.11n
    FIPS 140-2 mode supported       : Yes
    802.11w Management Frame Protection supported : Yes
    Hosted network supported        : No
    Authentication and cipher supported in infrastructure mode:
                                      Open        None
                                      Open        WEP-40bit
```

In this case, unfortunately, the Wi-Fi interface doesn't allow you to proceed with the configuration.

You can try replacing the Wi-Fi card with one that supports the feature, or you could try a USB Wi-Fi adapter.

In the event that the command output indicates a positive response, as in the example below, you can proceed with the configuration:

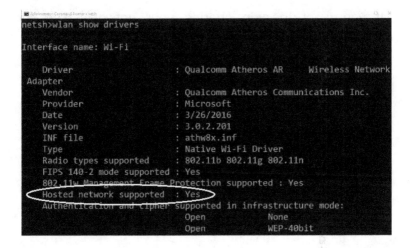

Type:

C:\>NETSH WLAN set hostednetwork mode=allow ssid=your_SSID key=your_Password

Your_SSID will be the name with which to identify your Wi-Fi network when you try to connect.

Your_Password, will be the one needed to authenticate users to your network.

After creating the network, you will need to activate it with the command given below:

C:\>netsh wlan start hostednetwork

If you want to stop sharing your network, type the following command and press enter:

C:\>netsh wlan stop hostednetwork

Chapter III   Various utilities: Open the "File explorer" window from the command line

To launch the "File explorer" GUI window, you can type *explorer* and press enter on your keyboard.

Wait a few moments and you'll be able to see the following window:

Duplicate the screen, extend the screen, or use only a second screen

To call up the graphical interface for managing the settings of multiple screens, you can use the **Displayswitch** utility.

```
C:\>displayswitch
```

After pressing enter, you'll see the GUI interface for managing settings, as in the figure below:

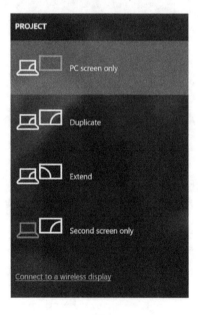

View a list of installed device drivers

The **Driverquery** utility can help you quickly view a list of the drivers installed on your PC.
Type *driverquery* and press enter.

Below, a part of the command output:

```
C:\>driverquery

Module Name  Display Name               Driver Type   Link Date
===========  ========================   ===========   ====================
1394ohci     1394 OHCI Compliant Ho     Kernel
3ware        3ware                      Kernel        19/05/2015 00:28:03
A38CCID      CCID USB Smart Card Re     Kernel        21/07/2014 05:26:27
ACPI         Microsoft ACPI Driver      Kernel
AcpiDev      ACPI Devices driver        Kernel
acpiex       Microsoft ACPIEx Drive     Kernel
acpipagr     ACPI Processor Aggrega     Kernel
```

The syntax of the command is shown below:

/S system   Specifies the remote system to connect to.

/U   [domain\]user   Specifies the user context in which the command is run.

/P [password]   Specifies the password for the user context.

/FO format   Specifies the type of output to display.
Valid values to pass with the parameter are "TABLE", "LIST" and "CSV".

/NH   Specifies that "Column Header" will not be displayed. Valid only for "TABLE" and "CSV" formats.

/SI   Provides information on signed drivers.

/V   Displays output in verbose mode Not valid for signed drivers.

/?   Displays this help message.

Expand the CAB files

The **Expand** utility allows you to expand one or more ".*CAB*" (cabinet) compressed files.

The syntax of the command is shown below:

EXPAND [-R] Source Destination
EXPAND –R Source [Destination]
EXPAND – I Source [Destination]\n
EXPAND – D Source.cab [-F:Files]
EXPAND Source.cab –F:Files Destination

The list below describes the elements of each row:

Source   Specifies the name of the compressed file.
Wildcard characters can be used.

Destination   Indicates the destination folder for the
unzipped file.
Destination can be a directory.
If the source is made up of multiple files
and –r is not specified.
Destination must be a directory.

-R	Rename expanded files.
-I	Rename expanded files but ignore directory structure.
-D	View list of files in source.
-F:File	Names of files to expand from a .CAB.

Activate the magnifying glass

Windows has a magnifying glass function to enlarge text in a file, images or portions of the screen.
To activate the magnifying glass, type the *Magnify* command.

After a few moments, you'll see the graphical interface to manage the enlargements.

Create a link to a directory, file or other partition

IMPORTANT: Before using the utility I am about to describe to you, I recommend that you make a backup copy of your PC because a program or the PC itself may stop working correctly.

The utility is *Mklink*.

Now I'll explain how to move a program from disk "C:" to disk "D:" creating a link between the two paths.

First of all, copy to a notepad the path where the program folder you need to move is located (ex. C:\Program Files (x86)\Adobe) because you will have to enter it in the command.
Copy the folder from the "C:" drive, cut and paste the folder containing the program onto the "D:" drive.
Check the new folder path on disk "D:" and copy it to notepad.
Open command prompt as administrator and type as follows:

C:\>mklink /j "C:\old_path" "D:\new_path"

Instead of "old path" and "new path" you will have to write the old path and the new path of the folder, which you wrote earlier in the notepad.
Press enter to complete the operation.

Now the junction between the two directories has been created successfully.

The syntax of the command is shown below:

MKLINK [[/D] | [/H] | [/J]] Destination link

The list below describes the elements of each row:

Link   Specifies the name of new symbolic link.

Destination   Specifies the path (relative or absolute) referenced by the new link.

/D   Create a symbolic link to a directory.
The default is the symbolic link to a file.

/H   Create a hard link instead of a symbolic link.

/J   Create a directory junction.

View the history of the commands typed

To see the history of the commands you have used since you opened the command prompt window, type the following command and press enter:

C:\>doskey /history

Below is the output:

```
C:\>doskey /history
ping
robocopy
title
doskey /history

C:\>
```

Open the command prompt from the "File explorer" window

If you browse through the graphical interface to the folder where you want to view the files via the command prompt, you can type "cmd" in the search field and press enter as in the example below:

In this way, the prompt window will open directly in the directory you need, without having to move through *"cd"* *(Change directory)* within the prompt window.

Shut down or restart a PC

You can shut down or restart a PC (both locally and remotely) using the **Shutdown** utility.

The reasons for which a restart of a PC is necessary can be many; hardware maintenance, rapid security correction, at the end of the completion of the installation of new applications, recovery/update of the operating system, etc.

The syntax of the command is shown below:

shutdown [/i | /l | /s | /sg | /r | /g | /a | /p | /h | /e | /o] [/hybrid] [/soft] [/fw] [/f] [/m \\computer] [/t xxx] [/d [p|u:]xx:yy [/c "comment"]]

/i   Displays the graphical interface (GUI).

/l   Does the log-off. You cannot use this command together with the option /m or /d.

/s   Shuts down the PC.

/sg   Shuts down the PC. You cannot use this command together with the /m or /d option.

After the system reboots, if automatic login on reboot is enabled, it will log in automatically and lock out the last interactive user.

After logging in, restarts all registered applications.

/r   Shuts down and restarts your PC.

/g   Shuts down and restarts your PC.

After the system reboots, if automatic login on reboot is enabled, it will log in automatically and lock out the last interactive user.

After logging in, restarts all registered applications.

/a   Aborts the PC from shutting down.

It can only be used during a timeout period.

Combine with /fw to clear any pending boot in the firmware.

/p Shuts down the local PC without waiting for a timeout period or sending an alert.
Can be used in conjunction with the /d and /f.

/h Puts the local PC into hibernation.
Can be used in conjunction with the /f option.

/hybrid Shuts down your computer and prepares it for fast boot.

/fw Combine with a shutdown option to have the next boot run in the firmware user interface.

/e Specifies the reason for an unexpected shutdown of the computer.

/o Move to the advanced boot options and restart your PC.
Must be used with the /r option.

/m \\computername Specifies a remote PC to shutdown.

/t xxx   Sets the timeout period before shutdown to xxx seconds.
Valid range is 0-315360000 (10 years), default value is 30.
If the timeout period is greater than 0, the /f parameter is implied.

/c "comment" Comment on the reason for the restart or shutdown.
A maximum of 512 characters are allowed.

/f   Forces all running applications to close without notifying users.
The /f parameter is implied when you specify a value greater than 0 for the /t parameter.

/d [p|u:]xx:yy Specifies the reason for restarting or shutting down the system.
The option **p** indicates that the restart or shutdown is scheduled; The **u** option indicates that the reason is user defined.
If the **p** or the **u** options aren't provided, the restart or shutdown is unscheduled.

The **xx** value is the main reason number (number with a value less than 256).

The **yy** is the minor reason number (number with a value less than 65536).

Move files from one location to another or rename files and directories

To move one or more files from one location to another, you can use the **Move** command.
The difference from other commands for copying files is that the *move* command does not leave a copy of the file in the source directory.

The syntax of the command is shown below;

Move one or more files:

MOVE [/Y | /-Y] [drive:][path]filename1[,...] destination

Rename a directory:
MOVE [/Y | /-Y] [drive:][path]dirname1 dirname2

[drive:][path]filename1   Specifies the path and name of the file or files.

destination   Specifies the new path to the file. The destination can include a drive letter followed by a colon, a directory name, or a combination of both.

If you only move one file, it will be possible also include a file name to rename the file while moving.

[drive:][path]dirname1   Specifies the directory to rename

dirname2   Specifies the new directory name

/Y   Suppresses the prompt to confirm overwriting an existing destination file.

/-Y   Shows the prompt to confirm overwriting an existing destination file.

Here are some examples:

To move the test.txt file from the current directory (\MKV\TX) of drive C: to drive E: (USB key).

C:\MKV\TX>move test.txt E:

Below is the output:

```
C:\MKV\TX>move test.txt E:
        1 file(s) moved.

C:\MKV\TX>
```

To <u>rename</u> the TX directory to Test:

C:\MKV>move tx Test

Below is the output:

```
C:\MKV>move tx Test
        1 dir(s) moved.

C:\MKV>
```

And here is the directory renamed from TX to Test:

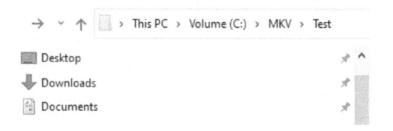

→ ∨ ↑ ☐ > This PC > Volume (C:) > MKV > Test

☐ Desktop   📌 ⌃

⬇ Downloads   📌

📄 Documents   📌

View the contents of a text file on the screen

To view the contents of a file on your screen, you can use the *Type* command.

Example.
To view the contents of the "Prova.txt" file, after positioning yourself in the directory containing the file, type *type* followed by the file name and press enter:

C:\MKV\Test>type Prova.txt

The command output is as follows:

```
Prompt dei comandi                                    —   □   ×
C:\MKV\Test>type Prova.txt
"Lorem ipsum dolor sit amet, consectetur adipiscing elit, sed do eiusmod te
mpor incididunt ut labore et dolore magna aliqua. Ut enim ad minim veniam,
quis nostrud exercitation ullamco laboris nisi ut aliquip ex ea commodo con
sequat. Duis aute irure dolor in reprehenderit in voluptate velit esse cill
um dolore eu fugiat nulla pariatur. Excepteur sint occaecat cupidatat non p
roident, sunt in culpa qui officia deserunt mollit anim id est laborum."
C:\MKV\Test>
```

Display date and time

To view the date, you can use the **Date** command and press enter:

```
Command Prompt                                          □   ×

C:\>Date
The current date is: Thu 11/03/2022
Enter the new date: (mm-dd-yy)

C:\>
```

If the date is correct, press enter again, otherwise enter the changes and press enter to confirm.

To view the time, you can use the **Time** command and press enter:

```
Command Prompt                                          □   ×

C:\>Time
The current time is: 15:51:15.13
Enter the new time:

C:\>
```

If the time indicated is correct, press enter again, otherwise enter the changes and press enter to confirm.

Delete a directory

To delete a directory, you can use the **Rd** or **Rmdir** (Remove directory) command.

Here are some examples:

To delete the "Test" subdirectory, type as follows:

C:\MKV>rd \MKV\Test

Below is the output:

To delete the MKV directory, <u>since it's not possible to delete the current directory</u>, you must move to the upper directory as in the example below:

C:\MKV>cd..

C:\>rd MKV

Below is the output:

```
Command Prompt                                                  — ☐ ✕
C:\MKV>cd..

C:\>rd MKV

C:\>
```

The syntax of the **rd** and **rmdir** commands is as follows:

RMDIR [*/S*] [*/Q*] [*drive:*]*path*
RD [*/S*] [*/Q*] [*drive:*]*path*

/S   Removes all directories and files in the specified
          directory as well as the directory itself. Used to
          remove the entire tree of a directory.

/Q   This option doesn't ask any user confirmation for
          removing a directory tree done with /S.

A more... kind command prompt!

I know the title puzzles you... yet the prompt is very customizable.

Instead of displaying the current directory followed by the "greater than" symbol (C:\>) you could enter a message to make it more... polite (for example: "Hi, how can I help you?").

To insert a message in place of the current directory, you can type the **Prompt** command.

Type as below and press enter:

C:\>prompt Hi, how can I help you?

Below is the output:

```
Command Prompt                                                    –  □  ×
C:\>prompt Hi, how can I help you?

Hi, how can I help you?
```

Since you no longer have visibility of the current directory, always use the _dir_ command to figure out where you are.

```
Command Prompt                                          – □ ×
Hi, how can I help you? dir
 Volume in drive C is Volume
 Volume Serial Number is 5C63-9456

 Directory of C:\

11/03/2022  11:16 AM    <DIR>          Intel
```

This output indicates that we are in the C:\> directory.

To restore the prompt to its original condition, type as below and press enter:

prompt pg

You can also edit the message, for example by "spreading" it over several lines.
For example, three lines of data (Time, date, current unit) and a fourth line where you can type the command:

It is 17:07:03.01
Today is 11/03/2022
The current drive is C
Your command:

To get this multi-line view, type the following command and press enter:

prompt It is t_Today is d_The current drive is n_Your command:

Below is the output:

```
Command Prompt                                           –  □  ×
Your command:prompt It is $t$_Today is $d$_The current drive
is $n$_Your command:

It is 17:07:03.01
Today is Thu 11/03/2022
The current drive is C
Your command:
```

Since if you make a mistake with a character or a space within the command, this will not work... I will report it below with the wording <space> which indicates to press the space bar once, leaving an empty space.

prompt<space>It<space>is<spazio>t_ Today<space>is <space>d_The current <space>drive <space>is<spazio>n_ Your command:<space>

and press enter.

To restore the command prompt to its original condition (as indicated above), type as indicated below and press enter:

prompt pg

Ex:

It is 17:07:03.01
Today is 11/03/2022
The current drive is C
Your command: ***prompt pg***

C:\>

Below is the output:

```
It is 17:07:03.01
Today is Thu 11/03/2022
The current drive is C
Your command:prompt $p$g

C:\>
```

Manage the label of a volume of a drive

You can assign, modify or delete the label of a volume using the **Label** command.
The command syntax is as follows:

LABEL [*drive:*][*label*]
LABEL [*/MP*] [*volume*] [*label*]

drive:	Specifies the drive letter to be changed.
label	Defines the volume label.
/MP	Specifies that the volume is to be treated as a mount point or volume name.
volume	Specifies the drive letter (followed by a colon), mount point or volume name. If the volume name is specified, the /MP switch is not required.

View the label of a volume

To view information about a volume (volume label and serial number) you can use the *Vol* command.

This command is useful when you are working on a machine with multiple drives (to which you assigned a label during the formatting phase), to make sure you are using the correct drive.

To check information about the unit in use, simply type *Vol* and press enter:

C:\>vol

The command output is as follows:

```
Command Prompt                                                  - □ ×
C:\>vol
 Volume in drive C is Volume
 Volume Serial Number is 5C63-9456

C:\>
```

The volume label (Volume) and the volume serial number are visible in the output.

For example, if you want to verify the information of another drive (for example a USB stick), type as follows:

C:\>vol E:

Below is the output:

```
C:\>vol E:
 Volume in drive E is FLASH DRIVE
 Volume Serial Number is 20B6-D4FA

C:\>
```

As in the previous output, the volume label (FLASH DRIVE) and the serial number are visible.

Adjust the repeat rate of a key

Using the command prompt, you can adjust the key repeat rate.

You may have requests from users who are particularly fast in typing on the keyboard, or who use the PC with videogames and / or appications that require very low response times.

Below is the complete command to adjust the speed:

C:\>mode con rate=25 delay=2

The **Mode** command basically uses three parameters:

con   In this case, it indicates the keyboard.

rate   Indicates at what speed the typed character should be repeated. The speed can be changed from the minimum value of 1 to the maximum value of 32.

delay Indicates the time to wait before the character is repeated.

The available options are 4:

- Enter 1 for a repeat delay of 0,25 seconds.
- Enter 2 for a repeat delay of 0,5 seconds.
- Enter 3 for a repeat delay of 0,75 seconds.
- Enter 4 for a one second repeat delay.

To realize the effect this command has, you can try to slow down the speed drastically, by typing the command with the parameters indicated below and pressing enter:

C:\>mode con rate=1 delay=4

Press and hold a single key to see how slow it has become.

If you also want to try the opposite extreme, type the following and press enter:

C:\>mode con rate=32 delay=1

Press and hold a single key again... the difference is noticeable, right?

To restore the keyboard to its original speed, type the command with the following values:

C:\>mode con rate=20 delay=2

Copy and/or replace existing files

The **Replace** utility allows you to copy and replace existing files in a destination folder with the upadted version of the same files in the source folder (The files must have the same name).
The utility also allows you to copy files from a source folder that are not present in the destination folder.

The command syntax is as follows:

REPLACE [drive1:][path1]filename[drive2:]
[path2] [/A] [/P] [/R] [/W]
REPLACE [drive1:][path1]filename[drive2:]
[path2] [/P] [/R] [/S] [/W] [/U]

[*drive1:*][*path1*]*filename* Specifies the source file or files.

[*drive2:*][*path2*]   Specifies the directory where the files are to be replaced.

/A	Adds new files to the destination directory. Cannot be used with the options /S o /U.
/P	Asks for confirmation before replacing a file or adding a source file.
/R	Replaces both read-only and unprotected files.
/S	Replaces files from all subdirectories in the target directory. Cannot be used with the /A switch.
/W	Waits for a disc to be inserted before continuing.
/U	Replaces (updates) only files older than the source file. If the destination file has the same date or a more recent date than the source file, this option prevents the file from being replaced. This is to avoid overwriting an updated file with an old file. Cannot be used with the /A switch.

Copy single files or entire directories

The **Xcopy** utility was one of the most used commands for copying files, until the arrival of the more modern and robust _Robocopy_ (which I talked about in the first book of this series about the command prompt) became part of the command line with Windows Vista and later operating systems.
The _Xcopy_ command has many options that allow you to keep everything under control during the copy process.

The command syntax is as follows:

XCOPY source [_destination_] [/A | /M] [/D[:date]] [/P] [/S
        [/E]] [/V] [/W][/C][/I] [/Q] [/F] [/L] [/G] [/H] [/R] [/T]
        [/U][/K] [/N] [/O] [/X] [/Y] [/-Y] [/Z] [/B] [/J]
        [/EXCLUDE:file1[+file2][+file3]...] [/COMPRESS]

source   Indicates the name of the file to copy.

destination   Specifies the path where "origin" is to
                        be copied.

/A   Copies only files with the archive attribute
                   set, without changing the attribute.

/M   Copies only files with the archive attribute
                   set and disable the attribute.

/D:*month-day-year*   Copies files modified after the
                   specified date (included).
                   If no date is specified, copies
                   only files whose source time is
                   newer than the destination
                   time.

/EXCLUDE:*file1*[+*file2*][+*file3*]...   Specifies a list of
                   files containing strings. In files,
                   strings must be reported on
                   separate lines.
                   If the absolute path of a file to
                   be copied corresponds at least
                   in part to one of the strings
                   present in these files, the file
                   will be excluded from the copy.
                   For example, if you specify a
                   string such as \obj\ or .obj, all
                   files in the obj directory or all
                   files with the .obj extension will
                   be excluded, respectively.

/P	Asks the user for confirmation before creating each destination file.
/S	Copies all files in the current directory and all subdirectories, except empty ones.
/E	Copies all files in the current directory and all subdirectories, including empty ones.
	Analogous to /S /E. This option can be used to edit /T.
/V	Verifies the size of each new file as the system writes it.
	It can be a very good option if you are copying important data and you want to be sure that it has been copied correctly, although it can slow down the execution of the Xcopy command.
/W	Prompts the user to press a key before starting copying. This option, in the past, gave the user the ability to insert a disk before starting; it can be useful when the amount of data is such that it's necessary to copy on more than one medium.

/C	Forces the Xcopy command to continue copying even in case of errors. (Normally the execution of the command stops by itself when an error occurs during the copy).
/I	If the destination doesn't exist and the copy involves multiple files, the destination is assumed to be a directory.
/Q	Doesn't display file names when copying.
/F	Displays the full names of the source and destination files when copying.
/L	Displays a list of files to be copied.
/G	Enables copying of encrypted files to a destination that does not support encryption.
/H	Copies also hidden and system files.
/R	Overwrites read-only files.
/T	Creates the directory structure without copying files. To include empty directories and subdirectories, specify /T /E.
/U	Copy only files that already exist in the destination.

/K	Copies the attributes. The Xcopy command without options resets the read-only attributes.
/N	Copies using the generated short names.
/O	Copies ACL and file ownership information.
/X	Copies file control settings (implies /O).
/Y	It doesn't ask for confirmation before overwriting an existing destination file.
/-Y	Asks for confirmation before overwriting an existing destination file.
/Z	Copy network files in restartable mode.
/B	Copy the symbolic link instead of the link target.
/J	Copies using unbuffered I/O. Recommended for very large files.
/COMPRESS	Requires network compression when transferring files where applicable.

View or change the system code page

You can use the **Chcp** (Change Code Page) command, to integrate the international keyboard and character set information, when you want to change the language or character set used by the command prompt.

To view the active codepage number, type as below and hit enter:

C:\>chcp

Below is an example of the output:

```
C:\>chcp
Active code page: 437

C:\>
```

In this case, the active code page is number 437. Corresponds to United States.

Code table

437 – United States
737 – Greek II
850 – Multilingual (Latin I)

852 – Slavic/Eastern European (Latin II)
860 – Portuguese
855 – Cyrillic I (Russian)
857 – Turkish
861 – Icelandic
863 – Canadian French
865 – Nordic (Scandinavia)
866 – Russian (Cyrillic II)
869 – Modern Greek
936 – Chinese

The syntax of the command is shown below:

CHCP [*nnn*]

nnn Specifies the number of a code page.

Type *CHCP* with no parameters to display the active code page number.

To change the code page, type *CHCP* followed by the three-digit code of the country / region or language you want to set and press enter:

C:\>chcp 865

If the code entered doesn't exist, the output returns the following message: "Invalid code page".

```
C:\>chcp 832
Invalid code page

C:\>
```

Delete the files

To delete files, you have two commands: **Del** or **Erase**.

Command syntax is shown below:

Del *drive:\path\filename*
Erase *drive:\path\filename*

<u>Both commands work the same way</u>, so all of the following <u>applies to both *Del* command and the *Erase* command</u>.

Below is an example of the output:

```
C:\>del C:\Documents\delete_test.txt
C:\>
```

In the example above, the "delete_test.txt" file inside the Documents folder has been deleted.

I recommend that you always use the **/P** option immediately after the file name, since in this way you'll be asked for confirmation before deleting the file:

C:\>del C:\Documents\delete_test.txt /P

```
Command Prompt - del C:\Documents\delete_test.txt /P                    □   ×
C:\>del C:\Documents\delete_test.txt /P
C:\Documents\delete_test.txt, Delete (Y/N)?
```

To confirm, type Y or N (Yes or No); if you press Y (Yes), the file will be deleted, but if you press N (No) the file will stay where it is. Then press enter to complete everything. This option helps prevent accidental deletion of a file.

Command options are as follows:

/P   It asks for confirmation before deleting.
          (Described above).
/F   Force deletion of read-only files.
/S   Delete the specified files from all subdirectories.
/Q   Non-interactive mode, dows not ask for
          confirmation for global deletions.

/A   Select files to delete based on attributes.

attributes R Read-only file   S System files
             H Hidden files   A Archive file
             I Non-indexed files   L Reparse point
             O Offline files   - Prefix to negate the
                                           attribute

If command extensions are enabled, the *DEL* and *ERASE* commands will be modified as follows:

The display semantics of the /S switch is reversed, as it only shows deleted files rather than those that cannot be found.

Configure a folder/directory as if it were a disk drive

The utility I'm about to show you is very handy and can make it easier for you to access a folder / directory without wasting time looking in a directory's hierarchies.
You can only perform this configuration via the command line, as it's not provided via the graphical interface (GUI).
The **Subst** (Substitute) utility allows you to configure a single folder as if it were a disk drive on your PC.
Here is an example in which you want to configure the "Test" folder to make it a "J:" drive.

IMPORTANT: After assigning the drive letter you have configured, you'll not able to use that letter for another drive (for example if you were to add a second hard drive to your PC).
I also invite you to check that the letter is not already in use by another drive (such as the "C:" drive).

Type the command subst, write the letter you want to assign to the disk drive (in the example below "J:"), write the path to the folder (C:\Documents\Test) and press enter:

C:\>subst J: C:\Documents\Test

The command output is as follows:

```
Command Prompt                                          -  □  ×
C:\>subst J: C:\Documents\Test

C:\>
```

To verify that the "J:" drive has been created correctly, type the command *subst* and press enter.
The command output will show you all the current virtual drives:

```
Command Prompt                                          □  ×
C:\>subst
J:\: => C:\Documents\Test

C:\>
```

Let's check on "File Explorer" what the Test folder looks like after the configuration in drive "J:".

As you can see from the image above, the "J:" drive is now easily accessible, as if it were an additional disk inside your PC.

To restore the previous situation, by deleting the newly configured "J:" drive (while keeping the Test folder inside the Documents folder) type as indicated below and press enter:

C:\>subst J: /D

The syntax of the command is shown below:

SUBST [*drive1:* [*drive2:*]*path*]
SUBST *drive1*: /D

drive1:	Specifies a virtual drive to which you want to assign a path.
[drive2:]path	Specifies a physical drive and a path that you want to assign to a virtual drive.
/D	Delete a replacement (virtual) drive.

Type *SUBST* with no parameters to view the list of current virtual drives.

By the same author:

- Stupidario tecnico: 101 frasi dette dai clienti all'Help Desk (Italian Edition)

- Come cercare e ottenere un lavoro: manuale per il successo (Italian Edition)

  How to look for and get a job: manual for success (English Edition)

- How to buy high fidelity: bring quality audio into your home (English Edition)

- The ultimate guide for speeding up your pc: go faster! Expert tips for top performances pc (English Edition)

- Windows 10 al Top!: Trucchi e strumenti per sbloccare il potenziale del tuo pc Windows (Italian Edition)

- Windows 10 da riga di comando: Guida rapida alla command-line di Windows 10 (Italian Edition)

  Windows 10 at the command-line: Quick reference guide to Windows 10's command-line (English Edition)

- Windows 10 da riga di comando Part II: Guida rapida alla command-line di Windows 10 (Italian Edition)

  Windows 10 at the command-line Part II: Quick reference guide to Windows 10's command-line (English Edition)

- Windows 10 da riga di comando Part III: Guida rapida alla command-line di Windows (Italian Edition)

- Windows 11: Guida pratica alle novità del nuovo sistema operativo Microsoft (Italian Edition)

- Windows 11: Practical guide to the latest Microsoft operating system (English Edition)

Riccardo would love to hear about your experiences with this book (the good, the bad, and the ugly).
You can write to him at:
windows10atthecommandline@gmail.com

* 9 7 9 8 3 6 2 6 2 2 2 7 5 *